AF270645

BASKETBALL
STRATEGIES

BY STEPH GIEDD

SportsZone

An Imprint of Abdo Publishing
abdobooks.com

abdobooks.com

Published by Abdo Publishing, a division of ABDO, PO Box 398166, Minneapolis, Minnesota 55439. Copyright © 2024 by Abdo Consulting Group, Inc. International copyrights reserved in all countries. No part of this book may be reproduced in any form without written permission from the publisher. SportsZone™ is a trademark and logo of Abdo Publishing.

Printed in the United States of America, North Mankato, Minnesota.
102023
012024

Cover Photos: Aaron Ontiveroz/MediaNews Group/Denver Post/Getty Images
Interior Photos: Beck Diefenbach/AFP/Getty Images, 5; Mitchell Leff/Getty Images Sport/Getty Images, 6–7; Preston Keres/The Washington Post/Getty Images, 9; Bettmann/Getty Images, 11, 42; George Frey/AFP/Getty Images, 13; Chris Coduto/Getty Images Sport/Getty Images, 14; Julio Aguilar/Getty Images Sport/Getty Images, 16–17; Al Bello/Getty Images Sport/Getty Images, 19; Focus on Sport/Getty Images, 20–21; Michael Hickey/Getty Images Sport/Getty Images, 23; Steph Chambers/Getty Images Sport/Getty Images, 25; Ezra Shaw/Getty Images Sport/Getty Images, 26–27; Denver Post/Getty Images, 29; Andy Lyons/Getty Images Sport/Getty Images, 32; Anucha Tiemsom/Shutterstock Images, 33; Ronald Martinez/Getty Images Sport/Getty Images, 34–35, 39; Shane Bevel/NCAA Photos/Getty Images, 36–37; AP Images, 41; Peter Aiken/Getty Images Sport/Getty Images, 44–45

Editors: Charlie Beattie and Patrick Donnelly
Series Designer: Joshua Olson

Library of Congress Control Number: 2023939419

Publisher's Cataloging-in-Publication Data

Names: Giedd, Steph, author.
Title: Basketball strategies / by Steph Giedd
Description: Minneapolis, Minnesota: Abdo Publishing, 2024 | Series: Sports strategies | Includes online resources and index.
Identifiers: ISBN 9781098292430 (lib. bdg.) | ISBN 9798384910374 (ebook)
Subjects: LCSH: Sports teams--Juvenile literature. | Teamwork (Sports)--Juvenile literature. | Athletes--Training of--Juvenile literature. | Basketball--Juvenile literature.
Classification: DDC 796.01--dc23

TABLE OF CONTENTS

INTRODUCTION

Since its invention in 1891, the game of basketball has gone through countless changes. The sport began with peach baskets as hoops. Its original 13 rules were tacked on a bulletin board. But those rules have been updated countless times. And that means players, coaches, and teams have had to adapt as well in order to keep up with the latest strategies.

At any level, fans look forward to the most exciting part of the game—scoring. Coaches are constantly drawing up new plays in search of baskets. At the same time, defenses get creative to stop opponents. Whether it's man-to-man or zone defense, everyone on the floor needs to be able to protect the hoop. Players who block shots, draw charges, and lock down top scorers make defense exciting too.

In basketball's early days, players were assigned to a position and stuck to it. Forwards and centers always played near the hoop. Guards spent their time away from the basket. In recent years, that's changed. Now a forward might be asked to shoot three-pointers and also grab rebounds.

Regardless of age or playing style, the team with the best strategy has a great chance to win. The most effective strategies today are a product of the sport's development.

Basketball is an exciting sport filled with action and strategy on both ends of the court.

SPALDING
JAMES
23
IGUODALA
9

CHAPTER 1

THE PICK-AND-ROLL

Chris Paul held the ball near the three-point line, staring down his defender while he waited for teammate Deandre Ayton to get into position. Ayton set up just to the left of Paul's defender. The 6-foot-11-inch, 250-pound Ayton planted his feet. That's when Paul made his move.

Paul, Ayton, and the Phoenix Suns were facing the New Orleans Pelicans in the first round of the 2022 National Basketball Association (NBA) playoffs. Late in Game 6, the score was tied 95–95. Paul and Ayton had

Deandre Ayton, *right*, sets a screen for Chris Paul during a game against the Philadelphia 76ers in 2021.

AYTON
22

been combining well on the pick-and-roll all game. Paul had yet to miss a shot.

With a quick step and dribble toward the lane, Paul brushed shoulders with Ayton. Paul's defender, Jose Alvarado, was a step behind. Alvarado crashed into Ayton's screen as Paul went around his teammate. Ayton then turned toward the basket. Paul now had two choices. He could pass to Ayton or take a shot himself. With two dribbles, Paul pulled up for a jumper at the free-throw line. Alvarado scrambled to get his hand up, but it was too late. The ball dropped through the hoop. The made shot put the Suns up 97–95 with just over seven minutes left.

The Suns won 115–109 to move on to the Western Conference semifinals, thanks in part to one of basketball's simplest offensive weapons. Paul finished the game a perfect 14-for-14 from the floor. He totaled 33 points, many of them off similar pick-and-roll plays.

SIMPLE BUT UNSTOPPABLE

The pick-and-roll is one of basketball's most reliable offensive plays. The strategy involves two players, typically a guard and a post player—a tall forward or a center, also known simply as a big. The guard dribbles the ball on the perimeter. The big steps up and sets a screen, or "pick," on that guard's defender. The guard then dribbles around the pick. Meanwhile, the big

Once the defender is screened, the ball handler has many options.

turns, or "rolls," into space and heads toward the basket. At that point, the guard has several options. What he chooses to do depends on how his defender reacts to the pick.

The defender might try to go under the screen. That means he moves between the screener and the basket. The route briefly moves him farther from the dribbler. If the dribbler sees that space, he can pull up for an open jump shot. But if the dribbler comes off the screen and no defenders pick him up, he can drive to the hoop. Alternately, if the screener is open on the roll, the dribbler can pass to him for a layup. The biggest advantage of the pick-and-roll is that it forces defenders to make tough decisions in the moment.

The play has even more options if the big is a good outside shooter. Once the screen is set, the big's defender may move to stop the dribbler's progress. This is called hedging. If the screener sees that, he or she can fade to the three-point line for an open shot or pop out for a quick mid-range jump shot. These variations on the pick-and-roll are sometimes called the "pick-and-fade" or the "pick-and-pop." With so many options off one simple move, the play is very tough to defend.

ITS BEGINNINGS

The pick-and-roll has been around since the early days of the sport. It was developed in the 1910s, approximately 30 years before the NBA was formed. Hall of Fame point guard Nat Holman is credited with popularizing the move. Holman played for the New York Whirlwinds of the American Basketball League (ABL) in the 1920s and later for the New York–based Original Celtics.

Nat Holman was one of the earliest players to adopt the pick-and-roll.

In Holman's book *Scientific Basketball*, he writes about the concept of "legal blocking." He describes it as intentionally causing one player to run into another and calls it "one of the most important factors in basketball." Today legal blocking is known as a pick or a screen. Holman called the pick-and-roll play described in his book "Execution Play No. 8." Though this strategy has been used unofficially since the 1910s, the pick-and-roll didn't get its name until the 1960s. It really took off as an effective offensive strategy during the 1980s, thanks in part to a pair of superstar teammates who mastered the play.

STOCKTON TO MALONE

Many of basketball's most effective duos have run the pick-and-roll well. But perhaps no one ran it better than John Stockton and Karl Malone. The two Hall of Fame players teamed up for the Utah Jazz for nearly two decades after Malone joined the team in 1985.

They made for an interesting pair. Stockton was a skinny, 6-foot-1, 170-pound point guard from Washington state. Malone was a sturdy, 6-foot-9-inch, 250-pound power forward from Louisiana. Despite their differences, their on-court chemistry was unmatched. Stockton was an

John Stockton and Karl Malone were a productive pairing for the Utah Jazz.

incredible passer. And Malone knew how to set precise screens. Once he got the ball, Malone was a dependable outside shooter. He was also nearly unstoppable in the low post.

Trae Young (11) looks to dish the ball to Atlanta Hawks teammate Clint Capela.

After setting a screen, Malone would read the defense. If his defender helped guard Stockton, Malone would slip away toward the basket for an easy shot. Malone could also quickly spin off the screen and seal off his own defender. That gave Stockton an open passing lane. Malone could then take a pass and drive to the basket. If the defenders caught on, Malone would pop out to the wing or corner for an open outside look. The two were so in sync on the court that Malone didn't always finish setting the screen before he made his next move.

The duo also played for a pick-and-roll expert—head coach Jerry Sloan. The trio led the Jazz to 14 straight winning seasons and two NBA Finals appearances between 1989–90 and 2002–03. Stockton retired in 2003 as the league's all-time assist leader. Malone played one more season with the Los Angeles Lakers. He was the league's second all-time leading scorer when he retired in 2004.

In today's NBA, players who can run the pick-and-roll well continue to be some of the league's highest scorers. The league began tracking advanced stats on different offensive plays in 2015–16. In 2022–23 point guard Trae Young of the Atlanta Hawks was among the best pick-and-roll ball handlers in the league. He averaged 11.9 points per game off pick-and-roll plays. That was nearly half of his 26.2-point season average.

Among post players, the best was Philadelphia 76ers center Joel Embiid. His average of 8.2 pick-and-roll points per game was nearly three more than any other post player. Embiid finished the season as the league's leading scorer at 33.1 points per game. He won his first Most Valuable Player (MVP) award after the season.

POSITIONLESS BASKETBALL

A trip to the 2022 WNBA Finals was on the line. Breanna Stewart and her Seattle Storm teammates were down 2–1 in the playoff series to the Las Vegas Aces. Stewart needed to have a big night to keep her team in the hunt.

Though the 6-foot-4 Stewart is listed as a forward on the roster, she has the skills to play both close to and far away from the basket. She showed that about four minutes into the first quarter of this playoff game. Stewart stepped up and knocked down a three-pointer to put her team up 10–7.

Breanna Stewart, *right*, is part of the new generation of players who are comfortable anywhere on the court.

Then, after her team snagged the rebound on the other end, Stewart dribbled the ball up the floor. She sprinted past her defender at the free-throw line and hit a running bank shot. A few plays later, teammate Gabby Williams grabbed an offensive rebound. Seattle point guard Sue Bird received the pass on the wing. She then passed it to Stewart, who made her second three-pointer of the night from the top of the key.

Stewart knows what it takes to be a champion. She won national titles in each of her four years with the University of Connecticut Huskies. Seattle then took her with the top pick in the 2016 WNBA draft. Stewart guided the Storm to a pair of championships in her first five seasons. She was hoping for a third during this sixth season.

Stewart's first-quarter outburst against Las Vegas was the start of a record-setting night. She finished with 42 points on 14-for-22 shooting. She hit six of eight three-point attempts. Her 42 points tied the WNBA playoff record.

However, Stewart did more than just score. She also had seven rebounds, two assists, and three blocked shots. The Aces outlasted Seattle for a 97–92 win. But Stewart had shown once again that she was one of the most versatile players in the league. Her style of play was a reflection of the modern style of basketball, which values players who can thrive anywhere on the court.

Stewart (30) took her skills across the country in 2023 when she signed with the New York Liberty.

OUT WITH THE OLD

For the first century of basketball's existence, most players had a set position. Each team's lineup included a point guard and a shooting guard. It also had a small forward, a power forward, and a center. Some players could move between two similar spots.

Each position also had a fairly specific job. Point guards were responsible for handling the ball and bringing it up the court. Shooting guards specialized in outside shooting. Small forwards played both inside and outside. Power forwards and centers stayed near the basket for close-range shots and rebounding.

This has changed, though. More and more players now can fill any position. One famous example of this was Magic Johnson during Game 6 of the 1980 NBA Finals. Johnson's Los Angeles Lakers were leading the Philadelphia 76ers 3–2 in the series. He was just a rookie that year, but he got his chance on the biggest stage. Starting center Kareem Abdul-Jabbar was out with an ankle injury suffered during the previous game. Johnson not only filled Abdul-Jabbar's role

Magic Johnson (32) of the Los Angeles Lakers showed he could dominate the game from any spot on the court.

LAKERS
32
SIXERS
53
21

as a center but also at various times played every position on the floor. As a result, he racked up 42 points, 15 rebounds, and seven assists. The rookie led the Lakers to a 123–107 win and the NBA championship.

As Stewart showed, that shift to positionless basketball applies to the women's game too. Post players are stepping out to take three-point shots. That takes their big defenders away from the basket. This in turn creates more room inside, allowing smaller players to get to the basket without worrying about their shots being blocked. Or smaller players can move inside and post up their defenders as bigs often do. Coaches realize that spacing on the floor creates many offensive options. But to do that, players must be versatile.

Former WNBA star Tamika Catchings started her pro career in 2002. The small forward became one of the sport's all-time great defenders before retiring in 2016. During

Tamika Catchings, *left*, was a great defender who also found plenty of other ways to help the Indiana Fever win games.

that time she witnessed firsthand how the game was changing. "When I was growing up, I remember everyone was put into certain positions," she said. "We don't have that anymore. The more versatile you are, the more opportunities you have."

At the end of each season, the league names its best players to the All-WNBA first and second teams. Those awards used to be given out by position. In 2022 the league changed that idea to keep up with the times. The teams now are made up of the five best players, regardless of position. League executive Bethany Donaphin said of the decision, "Our game continues to evolve. As a greater emphasis is placed on spacing and pace of play, the players have expanded their multifaceted skill sets." In 2022, the All-WNBA first team featured two guards and three post players. But the second team had four frontcourt players on it.

Stewart was named to the 2022 All-WNBA first team. She is one of the many players who have helped change the look of basketball. Elena Delle Donne is another. Delle Donne became an instant star in the WNBA after being drafted by the Chicago Sky in 2013. The 6-foot-5 Delle Donne won her first league MVP award in 2015. She won her second in 2019 with the Washington Mystics. That same year she led the Mystics to the WNBA title. Despite her height, Delle Donne is listed as a guard/forward on team rosters because of her varied skills. Scoring has always been Delle Donne's main strength. But she has also been an effective rebounder, ball handler, and passer. She continues to be a matchup nightmare for opposing coaches.

Elena Delle Donne launches a three-pointer during the 2022 WNBA playoffs.

Dynamic players such as Delle Donne keep opposing teams guessing. As a result, teams need to be able to play many styles of defense based on whom the opposing team has on the floor. Veterans who have adapted to positionless basketball continue to be successful in both the WNBA and NBA. And the players who haven't changed are left behind.

MOTION OFFENSE

The Golden State Warriors entered Game 6 of the 2022 NBA Finals with a chance to clinch the team's first championship since 2018. Behind superstar point guard Steph Curry, Golden State led the best-of-seven series three games to two. However, facing elimination, the Boston Celtics came out strong and led for most of the first quarter. Curry was determined not to let the game get away. With 56 seconds left in the quarter, he drained an off-balance three-pointer from the corner. The shot put the Warriors up by two.

Superstar Steph Curry runs the Golden State Warriors' motion offense.

Then Curry and the Warriors put their motion offense to work. Early in the second quarter, all five players lined up in a semicircle around the three-point line. They spaced themselves around the floor. Shooting guard Klay Thompson came off a screen on the right wing. Curry fed Thompson the ball at the free-throw line. Thompson nailed a jumper.

A few minutes later, the Warriors spread the floor again. With space to drive, Curry worked his way to the lane. After beating his man, Curry drew a second defender as he approached the basket. That left teammate Andrew Wiggins open in the corner. Curry passed to him, and Wiggins drained another three-pointer.

The spacing and constant movement of the motion offense gave the Warriors enough room to create and score from anywhere on the floor. And Golden State controlled the game from there. The Warriors' 103–90 victory wrapped up their fourth NBA title in eight seasons.

PLAYERS JUST PLAY

For much of basketball's history, teams ran set plays. Players had certain spots from which to start. Then they would carry out their specific jobs in the offense. As the play developed, players would look for opportunities to score. Over time, coaches started designing systems that were less restrictive.

Coach Hank Iba, *right*, was one of the inventors of the motion offense.

They let the players make more decisions based on what they saw. One of these new styles was called the motion offense.

Coach Henry "Hank" Iba and his assistant, Bloomer Sullivan, are credited with inventing the motion offense in the 1930s.

The pair coached the men's team at Oklahoma A&M, which later became Oklahoma State University.

At the time, a fashionable style of play was known as the "run-and-shoot." The simple offense was designed to move the ball down the floor quickly for a shot before the defense could get set. The rushed approach worked often, but it also led to bad shots. Iba believed his teams could slow things down and still get good looks at the basket.

Iba wanted his teams to get the most open shot possible. He devised the motion offense as a way to do that. His players were constantly moving and setting screens. They spent hours at practice weaving through the frontcourt and setting picks on defenders to create open looks for teammates. But it was up to the players to decide when to shoot. Whenever a great look at the basket popped up, a shooter could go for it. Iba called it "freelance with screens."

The Motion Mastermind

Hank Iba won 767 games in his college coaching career. That included 15 conference titles and two national championships. Iba also coached the US Olympic men's team three times. He became the first Olympic coach to win two gold medals in basketball.

Freedom became the theme of the motion offense. It was not about running one set play. Players were no longer told exactly where to go. Former Indiana University men's coach Bob Knight said of the offense, "We do not have an offense that involves patterns. I do not believe in teaching plays. I believe in teaching our kids how to make plays."

THE WRIGHT STUFF

To run the motion offense, teams start by spreading out. There are a few ways to set up the offense, including the three-out, four-out, and five-out sets. The "out" refers to how many players begin near the three-point line. A three-out formation will have three perimeter players with two others down low. A five-out setup has all five players outside. No matter how it is set up initially, the motion offense involves constant movement.

Former Villanova University men's coach Jay Wright started using the motion offense almost by accident. His Wildcats reached the Sweet 16 at the 2005 National Collegiate Athletic Association (NCAA) tournament. But in the second round, forward Curtis Sumpter suffered a serious knee injury. Wright didn't have a lot of backup options inside. But he had four talented guards. He decided to put them all on the floor at the same time. Wright brought backup guard Kyle Lowry off

Coach Jay Wright had plenty of success with the motion offense during his time at Villanova University.

the bench. The future NBA star joined starters Randy Foye, Mike Nardi, and Allen Ray in the starting lineup.

Villanova lost to North Carolina by one point in that Sweet 16 game. But Wright knew he was onto something. "We saw how it spread them out, how they had to chase us, how it opened up lanes to the basket," he said. The next year, Sumpter hurt his knee again. Villanova turned to the four-out motion offense. Wright's starting lineup had only one player on the floor taller than 6-foot-4. But Villanova finished 28–5. All four guards averaged at least 10 points per game.

His four-out motion became a go-to strategy for many coaches. Suddenly, teams didn't need much size. Every player could move and create space. And with no set plays, the Wildcats relied on their creativity. A player might pass to one wing, then immediately cut to the opposite side of the court.

SET IN MOTION

The motion offense spreads the floor and gives players many options to create open shots.

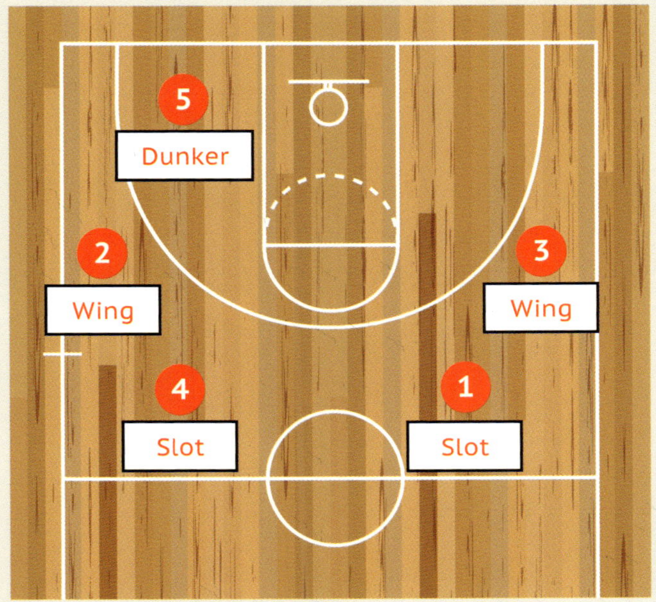

If that was not open, he could slice down the middle, looking for a pass in the lane. Other players could move to fill any open spaces. If the ball went into the post, that player could go up for an easy open shot. If the defense collapsed on him, he could pass out to a teammate for an open look.

Wright fine-tuned his system for the next several seasons. In 2016 Villanova won its first NCAA title in 31 years. The Wildcats won again in 2018. Wright retired in 2022 as a respected innovator of the game.

The motion offense also helped create more need for positionless players. Outside shooters especially thrive in the motion offense. In Curry and Thompson, the Warriors have two of the best three-point shooters in NBA history. Their ability to spread defenses out was a big part of Golden State's success.

Klay Thompson's three-point shooting helps keep Golden State's opponents on the run.

CHAPTER 4

UNDER PRESSURE

The NCAA basketball tournaments are nicknamed "March Madness." The Texas A&M Aggies were about to show why in the 2016 men's tournament. As a No. 3 seed, the Aggies were heavy favorites in their second-round game against the No. 11–seeded University of Northern Iowa (UNI) Panthers. But with 44 seconds remaining, UNI led 69–57. The underdog Panthers were surely headed to the Sweet 16. The Aggies hadn't given up yet, though.

After using 10 seconds to get to the other end of the floor and make a layup,

Texas A&M used a full-court press to get back into the game against Northern Iowa in 2016.

A&M
UNI
11
AGGIES

Texas A&M set up its press. One Aggie defender guarded the player making the inbounds pass, while four others played a 1-2-1 zone in the frontcourt.

The UNI player receiving the inbounds pass fumbled the ball. Texas A&M guard Admon Gilder picked it up. He dished it to Danuel House for an easy layup. The Aggies quickly reorganized to press again. Then the Panthers hastily passed the ball to a player near the baseline. Two Aggies swarmed. The heavily guarded Panther tried to bounce the ball off the defender's foot. But it was snatched up, and Texas A&M's Jalen Jones slammed it down for a dunk. UNI's lead was cut to 69–63, and panic began to consume the Panthers.

With 19 seconds to go, House made a quick three-pointer. Now A&M was down by only three.

Texas A&M players had plenty to celebrate after their pressure defense changed the game against Northern Iowa.

The press assembled again. UNI managed to beat the press with a lob to forward Klint Carlson for a Panthers dunk. But the Aggies came flying back the other way. Alex Caruso was fouled as he made a layup. He hit his free throw. The score was 71–69 with 11.8 seconds left.

The Panthers inbounded the ball quickly but were trapped in the corner again. Two Aggies closed in. Gilder intercepted the forced pass. His layup tied the game. The Aggies' incredible comeback was complete. The game went to overtime. Texas A&M went on to win 92–88. The Aggies' relentless full-court pressure had helped March Madness live up to its nickname.

CAUSING PANIC

The full-court press is not a new concept. John McLendon, a legendary college basketball coach and inventor of the fast break, was also responsible for creating the full-court press in the 1950s. Many college teams used the press successfully in the 1950s and early 1960s. But it was John Wooden who turned it into a true weapon.

Wooden coached the University of California, Los Angeles (UCLA) men's team. The Bruins' press was the envy of many coaches and teams in the 1960s. At that time, Wooden's teams usually featured average-sized players. But the Bruins executed the press well enough to fluster opponents into making mistakes and turnovers.

In the full-court press, the defense pressures the ball all the way up the floor. Other variations are three-quarter and

Coach John Wooden wanted his UCLA players to be ready to defend the court from baseline to baseline.

half-court presses. The simplest press is man-to-man. In that setup, each defender guards an offensive player all the way up the floor.

However, a zone defense features many press options. Common formations are the 1–2–2, the 2–1–2, and the 1–3–1. In each of these, the goal is the same: a pressing team tries

UCLA dominated the NCAA tournament during the 1960s and early 1970s, thanks in part to its pressure defense.

to get the offense to inbound the ball to a bad spot, usually a corner of the court. That way the defense can use the sideline and baseline as extra defenders, as Texas A&M did against UNI. Then the first line of players initiates the pressure. The players in the second and third levels move up once the ball is inbounded. The goal is to always have two players pressuring the ball. If the offensive player is cut off in all four directions, he has nowhere to go.

Wooden's teams used an aggressive attacking press called the 3–1–1. With three players pushed so far up, his teams created instant pressure. One player guarded the inbounder. Two guards protected the sides of the floor. But the most important player was the middle defender. One of his jobs was to predict where the first pass would go. Then he could move in for the interception. If the player with the ball held on to it, the middle defender could move up and trap while the other two frontline players dropped off.

Wooden trained his players to be in top physical shape. Pressing is tiring, and his players needed the stamina to keep it up all game. He also made sure UCLA could master the man-to-man press before working on the trickier zone version. That's because if the zone press was broken, the players would be able to fall back into a man-to-man defense before they were beaten for an easy basket.

Wooden's Bruins did this so well that during the 1963–64 season they went a perfect 30–0 and defeated Duke handily for the NCAA title. Wooden's teams didn't let up. Their constant pressing was a huge reason the Bruins won 10 championships in 12 years during the 1960s and 1970s.

In 2011, 33-year-old coach Shaka Smart took the Virginia Commonwealth University (VCU) men to the NCAA tournament. The Rams were a No. 11 seed. Not many expected them to go far. But playing a swarming press defense, VCU pulled off several upsets. The Rams even beat top-seeded Kansas in the regional final to reach the Final Four. By the end of the tournament, Smart's defense, which was nicknamed "havoc," was all the rage. It forced opponents to make quick decisions, which often led to mistakes.

Smart eventually moved on to coach the University of Texas. In 2021 he took over the program at Marquette University. A year earlier, the Golden Eagles had finished 13–14. Playing Smart's pressure style, Marquette reached the NCAA tournament in each of his first two seasons. In 2022–23, the Golden Eagles won a school-record 29 games.

GLOSSARY

assist

A pass that leads directly to a basket.

dynamic

Energetic and exciting; in sports, usually referring to an athlete with one or more outstanding skills.

execution

The ability to properly complete an athletic move or play.

perimeter

In basketball, the area near the three-point line.

pick

A legal block by a player against a defender to open up a teammate for a shot or a pass.

post

The area around the basket where power forwards and centers usually play. Sometimes the players who operate in this area are called posts.

trap

To perform a defensive play in which two players converge on the person with the ball to try to force a turnover.

versatile

Able to perform many different roles or functions.

veteran

A player who has played for many years.

Books

Flynn, Brendan. *Girls' Basketball*. Minneapolis, MN: Abdo Publishing, 2022.

Flynn, Brendan. *The NBA Encyclopedia*. Minneapolis, MN: Abdo Publishing, 2023.

Hewson, Anthony K. *Golden State Warriors*. Minneapolis, MN: Abdo Publishing, 2023.

Online Resources

To learn more about basketball strategies, please visit **abdobooklinks.com** or scan this QR code. These links are routinely monitored and updated to provide the most current information available.

INDEX

About the Author

Steph Giedd is a former high school English teacher and basketball coach turned sports editor. Originally from southern Iowa, Giedd now lives in Minneapolis, Minnesota, with her husband, daughter, and pets.